Gifted Children and Gifted Education

A Handbook
for Teachers and Parents

Gary A. Davis
University of Wisconsin

Great Potential Press, Inc.

Gifted Children and Gifted Education: A Handbook for Teachers and Parents

Cover design: M W Velgos Design
Interior design: The Printed Page
Edited by: Jennifer Ault Rosso

Published by Great Potential Press, Inc.
P.O. Box 5057
Scottsdale, AZ 85261

Printed on recycled paper.

10 09 08 07 06   5 4 3 2 1

Library of Congress Cataloging-in-Publication Data

Davis, Gary A., 1938–
   Gifted children and gifted education : a handbook for teachers and parents /
Gary A. Davis. — 1st ed.
      p. cm.
   ISBN 0-910707-73-1 (pbk.)
   1. Gifted children—Education—United States—Handbooks, manuals, etc. 2.
Talented students—Education—United States—Handbooks, manuals, etc. I.
Title.
   LC3993.9.D383 2006
   371.95—dc22
                                          2006008291

Contents

Preface

This condensed overview of gifted students and gifted education is intended for several groups—parents of gifted students, teachers of gifted students, "regular" teachers at any grade level, and other curious readers who did not take a three-credit gifted course in college. The book describes cornerstone components of today's school programs for gifted and talented students.

American education continually tries to help below average, culturally disadvantaged, minority, and physically impaired children become "more equal." Promoting *equity* is a long-standing virtue, and sensibly so. However, a widespread interest in cultivating the talents of our brightest and most talented students—promoting *excellence*—has been less consistent.

Some fear that gifted education will detract from educating our less capable students. Not true at all. We clearly must attend to students at both ability extremes—along with presenting a quality education of good breadth and depth to our in-between majority.

Of course, the futures of *all* young people are precious to themselves, their families, and society. At the same time, gifted and talented students will fill special roles. They are tomorrow's doctors, engineers, political leaders, authors, playwrights, business entrepreneurs, musicians, actors, producers, corporation presidents, and lawyers. Gifted students have special, often enormous talent to share with society. Their talent must be promoted, not squandered.

The present strong and growing enthusiasm for gifted education began in the mid-1970s. Federal statements, definitions, and a little money appeared. However, these improvements were short-lived. The marvelous 1993 report *National Excellence: A Case for Developing America's Talent*[1] summarized the vital need to support bright students and their critical role in America's future. The author's unforgettable two-word catch-phrase to describe the situation was "quiet crisis."

Problems continue. Currently, most states (not all) have enacted legislation that requires gifted students to be identified and to receive educational services beyond the regular curriculum. Some states (not all) supply extra funding to school districts.

Several noteworthy setbacks to gifted education have occurred. First, the mid-1980s "detracking movement" argued against gifted classes, alleging that tracking prevented many children, particularly minority students, from gaining access to advanced opportunities. Second, critics—who often are parents of "average" children—see gifted education as elitist, undemocratic, "giving to the haves," and diverting resources and attention to top students "who will make it anyway." Third, competency testing—as in today's "No Child Left Behind" policy—shifts the teaching focus away from an enriched and accelerated education for gifted students. Fourth, state laws and district policies sometimes are indecisive, at best. Fifth, when state or district budgets are cut, gifted programs are usually the first to disappear.

Often, school districts, principals, and teachers reluctantly create a gifted program only because of pressure from the state, the school district, or a group of organized parents of gifted students. It can be difficult to implement a program that equitably deals with minority, rural, handicapped, female, and preschool gifted students; rare children whose extraordinary IQs or talent are off the scale; counseling and technology in gifted education; and such common but routinely surprising gifted traits as high excitability, extraordinary sensitivity, and near-neurotic perfectionism.

Fortunately, today's enthusiasm for gifted education is high. The excitement is reflected in federal and much state legislation, and in the many successful public and private schools for the gifted. Gifted programs appear not only in America and Canada, but also in Mexico, Costa Rica, the Dominican Republic, Brazil, England, Scotland, Ireland, Italy, Bulgaria, Poland, Russia, China, Taiwan, Japan, Egypt, Israel, Saudi Arabia, South Africa, India, Indonesia, the Philippines, Guam, Micronesia, Australia, and other locations.

Why special treatment for bright students who probably "will make it anyway"? The following are goals and reasons for programs in gifted education:

To maximize learning, minimize boredom, and prevent the common college problem, "I never learned to study."

To satisfy psychological and social needs, mainly by meeting and working with other gifted and talented students.

To strengthen abilities related to communicating, independent study, and research.

To help students discover their gifts and potentials, thereby strengthening educational and career motivation.

To reward and strengthen individual interests.

To help students learn and think independently and take self-initiated action.

To teach students to think creatively, solve problems, and make intelligent choices.

In short, the aim is *to help gifted and talented students realize their potential growth and their potential contributions to self and society.*[2]

1
Gifted Students and Gifted Education

I consider this one of the most important of all problems
for the development of social science—the problem of how
to recognize, educate, foster, and utilize the gifted young.

~ Leta Hollingworth

[Scene: Hell. Devil with short horns, pointed tail, and dressed in red long johns sits behind a cluttered desk in his office filled with raggedy record books. A flickering Hellish fire illuminates the room. A sign on the desk reads "GIFTED DEMON PROGRAM." A proud and portly applicant enters.]

Devil (impatiently): Well, c'mon Sonny, we haven't got all eternity you know! What's your problem?

King Henry VIII: Sonny? Sonny? My good sir, I'm Henry the Eighth, former King of all England! I'm interested in your Gifted Demon Program. I assure you I am quite gifted at heinous torture and corrupt leadership. Besides, I've been boiling in fish oil for 450 years and I smell like an old carp. A change, good sir, would be most welcome.

Devil: Hmmmm. Look, Hank, we've got too many kings, queens, Kaisers, and caliphs in the program now! How about a transfer to Eye Gouging and Flogging?

Henry: Not really.

Devil: Well, Hank, what we really need are gifted troublemakers! How did you score on the Evil and Skullduggery Test?

Henry: Eighty-nine out of 100.

Devil: Not bad, not bad! Any special accomplishments? Sinister gifts? Villainous talents? Awards for diabolical evil-doing? Can you make college students come up two credits short for graduation?

Henry: Well, I've had six wives, beheaded two of them, and I tossed the Catholic Church right out of England!

Devil (smiling): Not bad at all, Hank! Actually, I like your style. Beheading's okay, but what you did to the Pope just tickles my tail! You're in! On your way out, would you send in the next applicant?

Henry: My pleasure, sir, and thank you so much!

(Henry VIII leaves. Cinderella's stepmother Rubella enters.)

Devil: Well hello, Rubella! How are things down on Brimstone V?

Rubella (noticeably upset): Oh, it just couldn't be worse, your Rogueful Royalty! All the time burn, burn, burn! My mascara is a mess, and look at my hands!

Devil: Glad to hear things are so infernal! So you're interested in our Gifted Demon Program? Wicked Stepmothers' Division, I assume?

Rubella: Oh yes, yes, your Sinful Sovereignty! I'm gifted at beating step-children and making them sweep up cinders! And I can be horribly cruel to Walt Disney's mice!

Devil (shaking his head): Not much imagination, Rubella! What about glitching computers? Causing accidents and fires? Starting wars? Sinking ships? How are you on debauchery and depravity?

Rubella: Sir! I have my morals!

Devil: That's what I was afraid of, Rubella. It's back to Brimstone V. Nobody ever said I was a nice guy!

Rubella (sobbing): But my eye shadow is streaking your Heinous Highness, and....

Gifted children are just that. A child's superior intellectual or talent capabilities are a "gift," not only to him- or herself, but to family and society as well. Such a child glows with promise for a successful and rewarding education and eventually a fruitful career and satisfying personal life. There may be three million such children in America.[1]

The child who is well above average in mental capability has many advantages, only some of which you may have guessed. But as we will see later, there also are problems, hurdles, and dangers. On rare occasions, even suicides.

Giftedness and Intelligence

Giftedness and *intelligence* are not synonyms, even though we can describe Einstein either as "highly gifted" or "highly intelligent." Of course, children and adolescents can be gifted in many different ways. For example, they might be outstanding students in all school subjects. Or they could be outstanding in a single area, such as mathematics or reading ability, but average in other areas. Or they could excel in drawing, playing the violin, or writing sensitive poetry, *with or without extraordinary intelligence.*

Today, *giftedness* in schools refers primarily to high general intelligence. In fact, as we will see later, many gifted and talented (G/T) programs are designed for students who are superior in intelligence/academic ability. Some states and school districts formally define *giftedness* as surpassing a specific IQ score. While other information typically is considered—and unless the candidate is a dedicated juvenile delinquent—a high IQ score is normally the admission ticket for a G/T program.

Most of this chapter will elaborate on the meaning and measurement of intelligence and the use of IQ scores in selecting students for G/T programs.

Intelligence

Smarter children learn faster, learn more, remember better, and apply knowledge more easily than children of average intelligence. Schoolwork comes more easily at all levels. So does every other aspect of life that demands thinking—making better sense of Hollywood movies, following instructions on doctor's prescriptions, staying out of trouble and out of jail, planning one's pre-college and college education, and thriving in one's career and personal life.

Long-time, world-class intelligence expert Arthur Jensen conceded that we can define *intelligence* in various ways.[2] He defined *intelligence* as the ability to induce relationships and correlates. Some of his research involved "simple" reaction time, in which subjects quickly pushed one button after a light signal, and "choice" reaction time, which requires choosing among two or three lights before pushing a correct button. He found that faster reaction times are related to other features of higher basic intelligence.

Of interest here: Jensen found the reaction times of highly intelligent 13-year-olds to be just as fast as the reaction times of university students—and a lot faster than reaction times of average 13-year-olds,

3

especially with choice reaction times. Jensen's simple research indicates that higher intelligence means that the brain in these individuals is more rapid, more efficient, and more accurate.

Intelligence is estimated by scores on intelligence tests, most of which produce IQ (intelligence quotient) scores. Intelligence scholars (like Jensen) use a small italicized g to abbreviate *general intelligence*, which refers to whatever is shared among intelligence tests.[3] In Jensen's words, "g is a distillate of what factors intelligence tests have in common."[4] Jensen noted that any individual IQ test score can only estimate g.

While we're dabbling in theories of intelligence, an interesting two-part theory considers g to be *fluid intelligence* (basic mental ability), which contrasts with *crystallized intelligence* (our accumulated information and knowledge). The distinction seems sensible; even Jensen likes it. The bad news is that fluid intelligence (g) begins to decline after about age 20. Logically enough, crystallized intelligence continues to increase.

Even though schools routinely administer group intelligence tests, IQ is best evaluated (estimated) by individually-administered intelligence tests. Individual IQ tests are simply more accurate and therefore a better basis for educational guidance and decisions, and school psychologists are trained to administer tests like the *Stanford-Binet Intelligence Scale* or the *Wechsler Intelligence Scale for Children* to individual children.[5] There also is a *Wechsler Preschool and Primary Scale of Intelligence-Revised*. Other intelligence tests are the *Cognitive Abilities Test, Henmon-Nelson Test of Mental Ability, Kaufman Brief Intelligence Test, Kuhlman-Anderson Intelligence Tests, Otis-Lennon School Ability Test, School and College Ability Test, SRA Primary Mental Abilities Test*, and the *Woodcock-Johnson Tests of Cognitive Ability*.

The Normal Curve

We need a brief refresher in statistics. The average IQ score for everybody is 100. The distribution, or "scatter," of IQ scores takes the form of a *normal curve*. So does height, weight, nose length, ability to do push-ups, and almost every other human characteristic or ability. The normal curve sometimes is called a "bell curve" because that's exactly what it looks like: most people are bunched in the high center, then the curve tails off in both directions, reflecting fewer and fewer people with progressively more extreme low or high scores (see Figure 1.1). Drawings always suggest that the normal (bell) curve never quite touches the baseline. But it gets extremely close.[6]

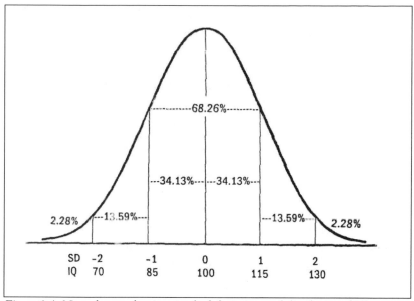

Figure 1.1. Normal curve showing standard deviations and distribution of IQ scores.

The normal curve usually is marked off in *standard deviation* units, starting at the center. For IQ, the standard deviation unit is 15 IQ points. From the average (mean) IQ of 100 to plus one standard deviation unit gives us an IQ of 115. (Was that difficult?) Minus one standard deviation is minus 15 IQ points, or an IQ of 85. Two standard deviations above (or below) the mean is IQ is 130 (or 70), and three standard deviations above (or below) is IQ is 145 (or 55).

Eight-four percent (actually 84.13%) of all people have a tested IQ of 115 or lower—that is, equal to or less than one standard deviation above the mean of 100. Ninety-eight percent (97.72%) have IQ scores of 130 or below—that is, equal to or less than two standard deviations above the mean.

We now enter the ozone level of IQ scores. Graphs of normal curves don't extend much beyond two standard deviations. You may think, "Why bother? Almost nobody's there." For your interest—and your child may fall into the next categories—an IQ of 145 is three standard deviations above the average IQ of 100 and is higher than 99.87% of everybody else. Percentage figures are not available for persons with IQ scores four standard deviations above the mean (IQ = 160), five standard deviations above (IQ = 175), or six standard deviations above (IQ = 190). Such persons exist, all crammed into that tiny top difference

5

between 99.87 and 100%. There is actually some evidence that there are more persons in this high level than the test scores indicate—perhaps substantially more than the normal curve would indicate—suggesting that the normal curve is not so normal after all, particularly at the upper end.[7]

Morelock and Feldman described children with extraordinary intelligence or other precocious gifts.[8] A few examples: at age four, Wolfang Amadeus Mozart composed a harpsichord concerto. At six, chaperoned by his father and sister, he toured Europe performing on the piano, organ, and violin. Michael Kearney is the youngest person ever to graduate from college—he was 10 years old. Two children—emphasize children—at age eight scored 760 out of 800 on the *Scholastic Aptitude Test*. Realize that just 1% of college-bound high-school students score 750 or higher. An 11-year-old female writing prodigy produced professional-level poetry that demonstrated remarkable spiritual, mystical, and psychological insights along with her creative use of language.[9]

Morelock and Feldman also sketched several persons with *savant syndrome*. Such persons are characterized by extraordinarily low IQ scores and minimal abstract reasoning ability but mind-boggling gifts in limited areas. See Inset 1.1.

Benefits of High Intelligence

Let's look at a few benefits of higher intelligence beyond faster, easier, and better quality schoolwork. Some will surprise you.

A study of men in the Australian military showed that deaths from auto accidents for men in the 85 to 100 IQ range was *double* that of men between 100 and 115 IQ. For those military men with IQ scores just a few points lower—between 80 and 85 IQ—the death rate was *triple* the 100 to 115 IQ group.

A study of Medicaid patients showed that illiterate patients racked up health care costs *four times* greater than persons of average intelligence. Compared with persons of moderately above-average intelligence (IQ 100 to 115), people of lower mental ability (IQ 75 to 90) are more likely to live in poverty, work at low-level jobs, and have many more crime convictions. They are four times more likely to have illegitimate children and 80(!) times more likely to drop out of school.

Research indicates that these profound differences are due to IQ level—not social class or parental influence; the same profound differences appear in siblings raised in different homes.

Savant Syndrome

Savant syndrome may be congenital or caused by injury or a disease in the central nervous system.[11] It occurs six times more often in males than females. "Savant brilliance" occurs in just a few areas: calendar calculating and lightning calculating (examples below), music (almost always the piano), art (drawing, painting, sculpting), mechanical ability, memory, and in rare cases, unusual sensory discrimination (smell or touch).

Consider identical twins George and Charles. Their IQ test scores were between 40 and 50. They could not count to 30, but they could instantly remember 30 digits. They became famous as calendar calculators, a talent that mystifies everyone. They could accurately answer such questions as "On what day of the week was your third birthday?" and "The year is 31275; on what day of the week will June 6 fall?" Given a date within an 80,000 year span, they could name the day of the week. For entertainment, they swapped 20 digit prime numbers.

Another savant, Kim Peek—like all savants—could not think abstractly or symbolically. When asked the meaning of "Follow in you father's footsteps," Kim said, "Hold Dad's arm so you won't get lost in the airport." When asked what he knew about Abraham Lincoln, Kim recited Lincoln's date of birth, date of death, how he died, Mrs. Lincoln's name, and his service in congress. Kim described Lincoln's Gettysburg address as "Will's House, 227 North West Front Street—but he stayed there only one night. He gave his speech the next day."

Higher IQ—*g*—of course leads to easier admission to college, college success, and eventual high-level occupations. One textbook illustrates the relation of IQ scores to careers by suggesting that persons with IQs around 83 might work in factories or restaurants or become health care aids or maintenance workers. We are likely to see persons of average ability (IQ about 100) as store clerks, security guards, or machinists. An IQ around 115 is typical of school teachers, accountants, and store managers. Becoming an attorney, chemist, or business executive usually requires thinking ability around IQ 127 or higher.[10]

But such relationships are not invincible. Many persons achieve occupational success well beyond these averages. High motivation and hard work can—*and does*—compensate for lesser ability. It's amusing that most successful people attribute their success to many years of diligent work and struggle. In fact, they're guilty of both high motivation *and* high ability.

High Spatial and Art Ability

While intelligence tests normally evaluate both verbal and spatial abilities, some tests evaluate just spatial ability. Tests of spatial ability require a person to, for example, figure out mechanical gear rotations or select the correct view of a rotated picture or design. One five-year study examined traits of 1,131 teenagers who scored above the 97th percentile in spatial ability.[12] Compared with lower spatial ability students, the high spatial ability students were more attracted to "ideas and things" and less attracted to "people and politics." In high school, they favored math and science courses, and they often planned college majors and careers in math-science areas. The research confirms our suspicion that math-science types are less social than others.

In the same research, one comparison of gender differences between high and low spatial ability teenagers produced a surprising contrast: on the *Strong Interest Inventory,* high spatial females showed the *highest* interest in art, but high spatial males showed the *lowest* interest in art. You may wish to speculate on the meaning and implications of this profound gender difference.

Regarding giftedness in art, Ellen Winner compared gifted art students to academically gifted students.[13] Both, she noted, are mentally precocious, think differently ("march to a different drummer"), and are driven by a "rage to master." With young gifted artists, however, IQ plays a small role. Indeed, some savants—by definition severely retarded—have been astonishing artists, noted Winner. But they do not draw at an early age, are more rigid, rarely draw people, and never become major creators.

Winner described one compulsive six-year-old who disturbed teachers by drawing during class and lunch. He had few friends—mainly because he only wanted them to pose so that he could draw from observation. Like other addicted young artists, he continually solved art problems—teaching himself to draw things as viewed from odd angles, things that were partially hidden, or things as they become smaller with distance. All at age six. He showed remarkable spatial ability and visual memory, but also remarkable reading problems and very little interest in school. However, he could name odd colors (e.g., fuchsia) when barely able to speak.

One gifted young girl could draw rapidly from memory (e.g., of a picture) and could begin her drawing at different points (e.g., at a dog's ear or tail). But her gross motor skills were so poor that she could not catch a ball.

Winner emphasized two important observations. First, schools do not support art talent. Second, art prodigies are rewarded for their imitative ability, not their creative imaginations. As the prodigies grow older, their routine efforts become dreary. They do not become eminent creators. Ideally, both artistic and creative talents should be reinforced.

Advantages and Problems of Intelligent Students

Leta Hollingworth is a legend in the gifted child field.[14] From 1920 to 1940, she pioneered gifted education in America, working entirely in the New York City area, and many of her 80-year-old observations and conclusions remain widely accepted. An especially noteworthy conclusion is this: students with an IQ in the "moderately high" range—about IQ 120 to 140—tend to be well-adjusted and successful in school. They relate well to other students, have close friends, and succeed at schoolwork.

Students with higher intelligence—especially those above IQ 180—typically have difficulties. They are too different, too smart to fit in. It's virtually impossible to find friends who share their advanced vocabulary and interests. An often-quoted statement by Hollingworth: "To have the intelligence of an adult and the emotions of a child combined in a childish body is to encounter certain difficulties."[15]

For example, one problem identified by Hollingworth is *emotional vulnerability*. That is, very bright children come to understand ethical and philosophical issues before they are emotionally prepared to do so—for example, poverty, starvation, war, genocide, and mistreatment of children. Parents must deal patiently and carefully with their child's emotional vulnerability to avoid long-term emotional problems.

Certainly, in regular classes, the smarter students get lazy. How can bright students retain high interest and motivation in a school environment designed for average—and below-average—students? They become idle. They daydream. They do not learn how to study. Many dislike school and find it a waste of time.

Hollingworth recommended counseling, which she labeled *emotional education*. Her recommendation remains paramount today. Counseling is now an integral part of every quality program for gifted students. We will examine counseling issues and strategies in Chapter 12.

Hollingworth's observations of social and emotional difficulties of bright students clearly contradicted some of Lewis Terman's earlier and well-known conclusions.[16] As background (continued in Chapter 2), the first successful intelligence test was devised in Paris, France, by Alfred Binet and Th. Simon.[17] In 1916, Terman extended, standardized, and published (in English) the Binet-Simon tests as the *Stanford-Binet Intelligence Scale*. Using his Stanford-Binet intelligence test, in the 1920s, Terman identified 1,528 children with IQ scores above 135, most above 140. His most famous conclusion: these children were above average psychologically, socially, and even physically.

The discrepancy with Hollingworth's findings probably is because Terman's students were hand-picked and recommended by teachers, who are known to select pleasant, well-adjusted "teacher-pleasers." Also, Hollingworth's comments stemmed from experience with *extremely* high-IQ students, considerably higher that most of Terman's 140+ IQ students, who were indeed likely to be well-adjusted.

In Hollingworth's footsteps, Miraca Gross more recently studied 60 Australian children with extraordinary IQ scores—all higher than IQ 160, with three over IQ 200.[18] Her students with IQs above 180 uttered their first word between six and 12 months and read fluently by age three. An Asian girl with IQ 165 could read newspapers at age two and medical books at four, graduated high school at 13½, and received a Ph.D. in theoretical physics at 21. One precocious girl confessed that she was not ready for college at age 13, so she repeated high school grades 11 and 12—taking different, more difficult classes—and entered college at 16.

Importantly, as children, those in Gross's study scored well *below* average on the *Coopersmith Self-Esteem Inventory*, and they knew that other students disliked them. Gross found that "school happiness" of high-IQ children related directly to their degree of grade acceleration. With no acceleration, these students held "a very jaded view of their education...they were negative and bitterly unhappy...they lost their zest for learning and achievement."[19] With one or even two years of acceleration, they still outpaced their new peers—but nonetheless were not particularly pleased with school. However, with *radical* acceleration (grade skipping two or more years), their schooling met their academic, social, and emotional needs, and they were delighted. Observed Gross, not accelerating an IQ 180 child is like placing a normal student in a class for the profoundly retarded.

Incidentally, note that bright peers are best found in programs for gifted and talented students. Self-esteem and school enjoyment always improve when gifted students meet others like themselves.

Today, the solutions of Hollingworth and Gross may seem obvious, and they lie at the core of virtually all programs for gifted and talented students. Such students need a motivating, stimulating challenge. Many programs include advanced work or enrichment beyond the regular curriculum. Independent library and other research projects are common. Several programs also accelerate students to higher grades. Many large cities provide entire public schools—called magnet schools—for gifted students. All of these options fire students' imagination, intelligence, and academic and career motivation.

Degrees and Kinds of Giftedness

Most elementary schools have some kind of special program for their gifted and talented students, although they usually are limited to students in grades 3 and above. Such programs unfortunately operate as though giftedness were a dichotomous capability. Children are either "in" or "out" of the program; they are either classified as "gifted" or "not gifted." Our normal, bell-shaped distribution of intelligence, however, illustrates that intellectual giftedness is hardly a "yes/no" matter.

Selection Policies, Procedures, and Considerations

Your author has never seen even two G/T programs that use the same criteria to decide who's "in" (gifted) and who's "out" (not gifted). Strategies and considerations for identifying students for a gifted program are sufficiently complex to deserve a chapter of their own (Chapter 4).

For now, consider a few basics. Criteria for admission to a gifted program usually include: (1) intelligence test scores, and/or (2) school grades, and/or (3) teacher recommendations. Teachers' recommendations are heavily influenced by a child's intelligence test scores and classroom performance, along with a teacher's impressions of the student's high motivation, intelligence, other strong talents, and even classroom behavior.

Schools also consider parental insistence that "I know my child is gifted! At home he/she is always...." Behavioral descriptions almost guarantee evaluation of the child, and parents usually are correct.

Also, consider these school policy and procedural differences. First, some states, school districts, or individual schools define giftedness strictly as *high intelligence*. A firm IQ number is set, normally 125 or 130, and all students scoring at or above this stamped-in-stone number are admitted to the program. From the school's point of view, such simplicity aids in both selecting students and arguing with parents who demand to know exactly why their "obviously talented" child was excluded. As a variation on a theme, some state or district policies allow the gifted committee of each individual school to set its own combination of selection criteria—but absolutely require that any student with an IQ score at or above, say, IQ 130 be included.

Second, regardless of which selection criteria are used, a school may specify a certain *percentage* of students who will be selected. The specific percentage, of course, exactly matches the available staff and space. The school G/T committee ranks students, and usually the top 5%—or sometimes a more liberal 15 to 20% (recommended by gifted expert Joseph Renzulli) are admitted.[20]

Third, in addition to evidence of general intellectual giftedness (IQ scores, grades, teacher nominations), a school may seek students talented in art, music, math, science, other art or academic areas, or general high-energy creativeness.

Incidentally, note that a student who works hard, perhaps guided and goaded by conscientious parents, will earn high grades and increase his or her chances of being selected. But high effort and parental praying will not influence the IQ scores produced by the Stanford-Binet or WISC tests.

Looking only at IQ scores, some students admitted to a gifted program will barely reach the cutoff score (e.g., 125 or 130). A few others will produce IQ scores of 140 or even 150—about the ceiling of today's IQ tests. A handful of other students scattered across the continent might score 180 to 200 on an earlier Stanford-Binet test. Despite obvious IQ differences, they'll all be put in the same G/T class together. One clear implication of this is that G/T teachers should help students select independent projects—for example, library research, science research, or art or community projects—so that students' projects will be coordinated with their capabilities and enthusiasm.

We not only will have differences in general intelligence among students in the same gifted program, we also will find differences in their interests, talents, and experiences. Some students in a program will be bright but bored with too-simple class work; others may be talented in creative writing, art, or chess; still others may show surprising depth in, for example, chemistry, magic, dinosaurs, cosmology, or history of the Revolutionary War.

Giftedness differs in both degree and kind. A sensible program for gifted students will be alert to both.

Admission Considerations

While varieties of admission policies and criteria will be discussed in Chapter 4, three preliminary comments are these. First, when a fixed IQ cutoff score is used, we could find the ridiculous situation in which an unmotivated and unimaginative student with IQ 130 is placed kicking and screaming in the G/T program, while an energetic, enthusiastic, and creative student with an IQ of only 129 is stamped "Not Gifted" and denied.[21] The need for flexibility is obvious. Creative and daring school G/T committees have ignored the state or district cutoff scores to admit the more promising and enthusiastic IQ 129 kid. It's a certain bet that he or she will become a more productive contributor to society than the less motivated student with one more IQ point.

Second, Joseph Renzulli's influential three-part definition of giftedness includes *motivation, creativity,* and at least *above-average intelligence.* While the tested IQ scores of some eminent creative and productive people are very high, many show IQ scores at or slightly above just 120. Simonton argued that America's most creative and productive people—at least those who do not require an M.D., LL.B., or Ph.D. for their profession—often do not even finish college.[22] Many complete just two and a half or three years of college, but they have the high creativity and strong motivation essential to their success and later eminence.

Third, we noted that some programs set a fixed percentage of students who are admitted. The top 5% is common. We also noted that Renzulli and Reis's increasingly popular strategy is to admit a more liberal 15 to 20%.[23] When in doubt, admit. With a higher percentage admitted, more students will receive advanced work and enrichment experiences. And a higher admission percentage virtually eliminates parent complaints that their (obviously brilliant and talented) child was unfairly excluded.

13

For School Success: High Intelligence and High Effort

Of course, schoolwork is easier for smart kids. But they still must work. School success should never be automatic, even for high-ability students. If you are a parent, does your capable child have good study habits? Do you communicate clearly to your child the firm relationship between hard work and success? Do you show a clear interest in your child's school success? Do you volunteer at school? Do you speak with your child's teacher whenever you can? Do you monitor homework, ensuring that it is not second banana to TV?

Parents, you absolutely must demonstrate to your child that you value school and classroom achievement—including regular and successful homework—that corresponds to your child's capability.

Types of Giftedness

Intelligence, Creativity, Motivation

We agree that high basic intelligence—g—is a sensible criterion of giftedness. We also know that people, including children, differ from one another. They have different interests, different capabilities, different levels of motivation, and more. Pablo Picasso is a nice example. Every tutor who tried to teach little Pablo to read gave up in frustration. When he reached the age of nine, his father quit hiring tutors. At age 14, Picasso painted like Rembrandt, but he could only just write his name. Albert Einstein, also dyslexic, did not learn to read until age eight.

The point is that basic intelligence—estimated with IQ scores—is only one form of giftedness. As noted in Renzulli's definition of giftedness, creativity is another important gift. Some high IQ kids might never have had an original idea in their young lives. Other students, who may have lower IQ scores, might be marvelous artists, writers, poets, musicians, or backyard tinkerers and inventors. Renzulli's third component of giftedness—motivation, high interest, enthusiasm—will certainly help determine future educational and career success.

The above are good reasons why teacher recommendations are important. The teacher probably is aware of a student's unique gift that deserves encouragement and opportunity to blossom, and he or she certainly is aware of students with high motivation and energy.

With all this in mind, is it reasonable to base admission strictly on an IQ cutoff score?

Standardized Achievement Test Scores

Scores on nationally standardized achievement tests (discussed further in Chapter 4) are another common admission criterion. *Nationally standardized* means that the academic achievement level of students in Randolph, Utah, (population 483) may be compared with the achievement of same-age students in cities like Boston, Miami, Omaha, Seattle, Honolulu, and Fairbanks. Therefore, a teacher who examines the nationally standardized achievement test norms can determine immediately if a high-achieving third-grade student also rates high in comparison with other third-graders across the country. It's not just that the student looks gifted in comparison with dull-witted classmates.

The most frequently used standardized tests are the *Metropolitan Achievement Tests, Iowa Tests of Basic Skills, Stanford Achievement Tests, SRA Achievement Series, California Test of Basic Skills,* and *Sequential Tests of Educational Progress.* Every elementary school in the nation almost certainly uses one of these. These various tests evaluate slightly different academic areas and subareas and have different time requirements.

Like IQ tests, achievement tests will *not* identify the child as talented in music, art, social skills, creativity, leadership, entrepreneurship, or organization (getting things done) talent.

Beyond Single IQ Scores

Two contemporary and refreshing theories emphasize that picking children for a G/T program based on a single IQ number is…well, not only unreasonable and unfair, but borderline bizarre.

Chapter 3 explores theories and definitions of giftedness. It reviews Howard Gardner's theory of multiple intelligences. Gardner's most recent version currently includes eight (up from seven) types of intelligence—*only two of which, linguistic and logical-mathematical, are valued by educators and routinely used in selecting children for G/T programs.*[24] Other important forms of intelligence described by Gardner include, for example, musical, bodily-kinesthetic, and interpersonal intelligence, all of which are ignored by most G/T selection committees.

In a thought-provoking distinction, Robert Sternberg described just three types of intelligence.[25] *Analytic* intelligence—like Gardner's linguistic and logical-mathematical intelligence—is measured by IQ tests and is used by educators. Sternberg's *creative* intelligence and *practical* intelligence (successfully applying creative and analytic intelligence to everyday situations), although equally or more important, may be ignored by educators, particularly practical intelligence.

Gifted Consultants, Teachers of the Gifted, and School G/T Committees

A *gifted consultant* typically is a teacher who works for the district, has taken coursework in gifted education, and may have a master's degree in gifted education.[26] The gifted consultant's usual job, first, is to help individual schools establish their gifted programs. Second, they travel from school to school during the week to teach small groups of gifted children in pullout programs. The structure and content of most types of gifted programs will be elaborated in later chapters, but briefly, the consultant will teach creativity and thinking skills (e.g., critical thinking, reasoning, analyzing, planning, evaluating, and hundreds more) and help plan and direct independent student projects, usually library or scientific research projects, sometimes school or community (e.g., science fair) projects.

In contrast, a school's *teacher of the gifted*, commonly abbreviated "gifted teacher," may or may not have taken coursework in gifted education. Based on high interest, apparent qualifications, availability, and sometimes just close friendship with a principal who underestimates the importance of the job, the gifted teacher usually teaches either: (1) a multi-age pullout group of gifted students who meet for two or three hours on Wednesday afternoons, or (2) a full-time classroom of multi-age gifted students.

Ideally, if not in common practice, each school will have a G/T committee. The committee will include the district's gifted consultant, the school's gifted teacher, the principal or other administrator, and one or more parents of gifted children. The committee, ideally, will consult the 1998 National Association for Gifted Children's (NAGC) *Pre-K–Grade 12 Gifted Program Standards*.[27] These standards present sensible identification procedures, enrichment and acceleration activities, and program evaluations. The committee will create a written program plan so that interested parents and other persons (e.g., central administrators, other schools) will know exactly *what* the G/T program intends to do and *how, why*, and *for whom*. The district will then print and distribute a brochure describing the gifted program so that parents and others will know what services are offered.

Yes, ideally.

Equity or Excellence?

We commented in the Preface on America's "love-hate" relationship with gifted students. On one hand, we admire bright children who rise from modest backgrounds to high educational and professional success. But many people—too many, it seems—look at programs for the gifted as elitist, undemocratic, and giving to the "haves" while ignoring the "have nots." We might hear such comments as "Those kids will make it on their own" and "Give the help to kids who need it!"

The political pendulum continues to swing—as it has for many years—between strong support for *excellence* versus an even stronger concern for *equity*. The solution is simple. It is not an either/or decision. *We need both.* Slower-learning students—including those with emotional or physical disabilities, different language and cultural backgrounds, as well as those with low intellectual capacity—obviously need special educational help, and they should receive it. But bright students also have unique needs and problems, and they also should receive special educational assistance and programs to help them reach their potential.

Detrimental Educational Policies: Detracking, Competency Testing, and Cooperative Learning

As final introductory comments, we should mention the detracking movement, national and state proficiency testing, and cooperative learning, which were also noted in the Preface.

Detracking Movement

"Tracking" refers to grouping students by ability. For example, a large elementary school might have five fifth-grade classrooms—one for low, three for average, and one for above-average students. High schools will have algebra and beginning chemistry classes for some students, and pre-college calculus and organic chemistry for others. But a troublesome detracking, anti-grouping effort became popular largely because of Jeanie Oakes' 1985 book *Keeping Track*.[28] Oakes and her cohorts argued that tracking is: (1) racist because it places too many minority students in slower tracks, (2) damaging to the self-concepts of low-track students, and (3) unfair because it denies some students access to advanced content and opportunity. She also claimed that tracking produced no academic benefit.

Mara Sapon-Shevin's 1994 book entitled *Playing Favorites: Gifted Education and the Disruption of Community* did not help either. Nor did a 1981 book by well-known developmental psychologist David Elkind entitled *The Hurried Child: Growing Up Too Fast Too Soon,* which claimed that children can be harmed by pushing them too fast for their developmental level.

The combined result was wholesale trashing of educational tracking—at least at the elementary school level. An immediate effect was that the self-concepts of below-average children *worsened* because they now competed with brighter children.[29] Unfortunately, many schools also terminated their gifted programs—easily viewed as "tracking"— and bright students once again found themselves twiddling their thumbs waiting for other students to grasp what they had known and understood for at least one or two years.

Fortunately, gifted education survived the detracking threat and is now growing worldwide. In fact, a noteworthy benefit—yes, benefit—of the detracking movement was to bring some gifted education teaching strategies into the regular classroom, particularly the teaching of creativity and other higher-level thinking skills. Note the title of Joseph Renzulli and (wife) Sally Reis's book *The Schoolwide Enrichment Model,*[30] and Renzulli's book *Schools for Talent Development: A Practical Plan for Total School Improvement.*[31]

As another happy note on detracking *non*-damage, Governor's School summer programs (Chapter 6) and private and magnet schools for the gifted (Chapter 7) were not affected by the Oakes et al. attack—due no doubt to their obvious high success in educating gifted students.

National and State Competency Testing

Many teachers try to accommodate the needs of gifted students in their regular classroom (in some cases because Jeanie Oakes' publications led to the termination of the school's gifted program). For example, a gifted-conscious teacher might help gifted students explore independent research or art projects, perhaps with a learning contract that outlines the details of the project, its duration, and the form of the final report or product.[32]

Now imagine that this teacher's principal emphatically reminds every teacher that state competency tests—which assess basic skills and knowledge appropriate for each grade level—will be administered to all students in a few months. The message from this administrator is that every child damn well better pass, and the higher the children's scores, the better. The principal might remind teachers that: (1) the school's average competency test performance will appear in newspapers all over the state—clearly ranked in comparison with other schools, (2) the principal does not wish to look incompetent, and (3) any teacher whose students produce low scores on the competency test will be fired.

The principal is serious. To prevent slow students from cutting class on the day of tests—an earlier stunt encouraged by wily teachers—high attendance on test day is required. Ninety-five percent of the school's students must take the tests or the school "fails," regardless of how high the test-taking students—perhaps 94% the school's students—score on the tests.

According to Robert Brennan, Professor of Education at the University of Iowa, the federal *No Child Left Behind Act* (NCLB) might better be worded as the *Most Children Left Behind Act*.[33] The Act focuses obviously on educationally disadvantaged students—students who are below average in ability, are economically disadvantaged, are members of major racial/ethnic groups, have disabilities, or have limited English ability. *The NCLB Act shows zero concern for the educational problems of gifted—or even average—students.* As of 2003-2004, the "outrageously unrealistic" Iowa regulations (all states differ) require that every student in grades 3 through 8 and in one high school grade will be tested annually in reading/language arts and mathematics. In Iowa, annual tests in science begin in 2007-2008.

The use of such tests is not without controversy, however. There have been court cases concerning racial discrimination related to high school graduation tests (basic skills tests that may prevent graduation), as well as about IQ testing with educable mentally retarded students.

Cooperative Learning

The term *cooperative learning* refers to small groups of students—usually about four—who work together to help each other learn. Sometimes the groups deliberately are composed of students at different ability levels—for example, two medium ability, one high ability, and one low ability who is perhaps retarded or has a learning disability.

The overall effect has been remarkably successful. Motivation and achievement run high. Students learn to communicate clearly. Group discussions aid thinking skills, such as asking good questions, considering others' ideas, and avoiding too-rapid decisions. Some educators recommended cooperative learning as the primary instructional method, especially for teaching reading, writing, and math.[34]

19

The problem should be obvious—everybody benefits except gifted students, who find themselves in the role of "junior teacher." They get stuck doing most of the work. They miss opportunities for suitable acceleration and enrichment. They almost always would prefer not to work in such groups. And they lose school motivation.

Misuses of Gifted Children

As a final note, consider three common and "classic misuses of gifted children in our education system."[35] First, teachers often have gifted students tutor slower-achieving students. This is fine for the slow students, but the bright kids learn nothing—except how to tutor slow learners. Second, because gifted students complete their work early, some teachers assign *grade-level* enrichment (at best) or busy-work (at worst) to keep the bright students occupied while slower classmates finish their work. The third misuse of gifted students, quite honestly, can be a common problem in accommodating their high abilities: assigning more and harder work can be "a punishment for being bright."[36]

Summary

- Children may be gifted in many ways, but giftedness refers most strongly to general intelligence. Some states define *giftedness* as surpassing a given IQ score.

- Arthur Jensen found that faster reaction times relate to higher intelligence—that is, a brain that is faster, more efficient, and more accurate.

- General intelligence—g—is estimated by intelligence tests.

- Fluid intelligence is basic mental ability. Crystallized intelligence is accumulated knowledge.

- Individual intelligence tests—the Stanford-Binet and WISC—are more accurate than group tests.

- The normal curve illustrates the distribution of IQ scores. One hundred is average, with a standard deviation of 15 IQ points. Ninety-eight percent of the population will have IQ scores below 130.

- Persons with lower intelligence have more auto accidents, run up higher Medicaid bills, and are more likely to live in poverty, have low-level jobs, have crime convictions, and drop out of school. High motivation can compensate for lesser ability.

- Teenagers with high spatial ability are more attracted to "ideas and things" and less attracted to "people and politics." High spatial ability females, but not males, show strong interest in art.

- Morelock and Feldman described children with extremely high intelligence or other amazing gifts—for example, Mozart. Savant syndrome refers to retarded persons who display unexplainable gifts in calendar calculating, music (piano), art, mechanical ability, or memory.

- With gifted artists, IQ plays a small role. Winner concluded that schools do not support art talent, and art prodigies are rewarded for their imitative ability, not creativity.

- Hollingworth concluded that students with IQs of about 120 to 140 are well adjusted, but students with higher IQs have social and emotional difficulties. "Emotional vulnerability" means that bright children understand such issues as poverty and war before they can cope emotionally. In regular classes, bright students become lazy. Hollingworth recommended *emotional education*, i.e., counseling.

- Terman's high IQ students were above average psychologically, socially, and physically.

- With children over IQ 160, Gross found that "school happiness" related directly to their amount of grade acceleration.

- Many large cities have special magnet schools for the gifted.

- Different gifted programs use different selection criteria, usually including IQ scores, grades, and/or teacher recommendations. Parent input is important and influential.

- Some schools require a minimum IQ score for admission to a G/T program. Some set a fixed percentage of students. Other schools select students talented in art, music, math, energetic creativeness, etc.

- Students in the same program may vary dramatically in intelligence, as well as in specific talents.

- A firm IQ cutoff can discriminate against a student with a slightly lower IQ but much higher creativity and motivation.

- Renzulli's definition of giftedness includes high creativity, high motivation, and above-average intelligence.

- Renzulli's recommended admission policy for gifted programs is 15 to 20% of students.

- Parents should show their children that they value education and hard work.

- Simonton noted that many creatively productive people do not finish college.

- Creative persons Picasso and Einstein were dyslexic.

- Standardized achievement test scores permit comparison of students in all parts of the U.S.

- Both Gardner and Sternberg propose looking at several forms of intelligence.

- A *gifted consultant* normally has training in gifted education, works for the district, helps establish G/T programs, and teaches in pullout plans. A *teacher of the gifted*, or "gifted teacher," typically instructs pullout students or special gifted classes.

- Some schools have G/T committees, consisting of an administrator, the gifted teachers, and parents. Such committees should consult the NAGC Gifted Program Standards.

- America has a "love-hate" relationship with the gifted. Some complain that programs are elitist and undemocratic. A country needs both educational equity and excellence.

- The 1985 Jeanie Oakes detracking movement led to terminating many gifted programs. The movement also led to incorporating some gifted teaching strategies (creativity, thinking skills) into the regular classroom.

- Governor's Schools and private school programs were unaffected by the detracking movement.

- Competency testing shifts the educational focus to below-average students and away from average and gifted students.

- With cooperative learning, gifted students become teachers, do most of the work, and miss opportunities for accelerated work.

- Some teachers use gifted students as tutors or assign them busy-work. A dilemma is that assigning more and harder work may be a punishment for being gifted.

2
Characteristics of the Gifted

While some gifted children are naturally cooperative and
easy going, other equally bright children [are] feisty,
challenging, and strong-willed.

~ Deborah L. Ruf

[*Scene: Harriet Brush, Queen of American Education, has just ended a speech to a group of teachers in which she has presented her new educational theory. With a confident smile, she asks if anyone has a question.*]

Teacher Abby Jones (with tilted head and screwed up face): Your Highness, under your new plan, *Every Child Left Behind*, would you tell us again about state competency tests? I'm not sure I believe what I heard.

Queen Harriet Brush: As I explained, it's terribly unfair for bright students to earn high grades, go to college, and become doctors, lawyers, and business leaders while other students struggle with simple reading and arithmetic. They become frustrated, drop out of school, and find only low-paying jobs. It happens all the time!

Teacher Jones: And your solution was…?

Queen Brush (seriously): Every state must administer competency tests after grades 2, 5, 8, and 11. Any student who scores high is excluded from further education. Each school will create a large TV room where bright, fast-learning children can watch cartoons, Oprah, and reruns of Dallas Cowboys games! With my plan, all students will achieve at exactly the same level! It's only fair. (Her confident smile returns.)

(Teacher Jones collapses in her seat, head in her hands, crying.)

Teacher Rhonda Sterling: Your Highness, I teach math and algebra in a middle school. Does your plan mean that I will be teaching only students who can't add and subtract? My bright math kids won't be there?

Queen Brush (smiling even wider): That's absolutely correct! No more show-offs in math, physics, chemistry, or advanced literature! My plan will totally eliminate these awful differences in achievement. This is America, land of equality!

Teacher Jackie Shorts: Excuse me. I'm Jackie Shorts. I teach physical education for girls and coach the girls' track team. We just do calisthenics, play soccer and softball, and my track kids run. Nothing you've said will affect my classes or the track team, right?

Queen Brush (seriously): Oh not so fast, Jockie!

Teacher Shorts: That's Jackie.

Queen Brush: That's what I said—please pay attention. Now, Jockie, with my inspired...(she pauses in self-admiration) and visionary... (pauses again) plan, we must eliminate unfair, un-American advantages of some students, including their athletic ability. My plan is brilliantly simple! (Pauses, tilts head, smiles to herself.) Faster students will wear ankle weights, and the faster the student, the heavier the weight. It's so simple! (Pauses, smiles.) And again, everyone will be equal—the American dream!

Teacher Alex Wunderland: But your Majesty, our graduation requirements! Will *anyone* meet them? Will *anyone* graduate?

Queen Brush: Of course! *All* students will graduate! *All* students will be equally competent. It's so fair and...and American! (Pauses, smiles.)

Teacher Wunderland: But if no one learns, how will anyone meet graduation requirements?

Queen Brush: Easy! You must have missed my explanation. We eliminate graduation requirements. There's no need for them. Everyone's equal. So everyone graduates! My plan is...well...so inspired! (Pauses, with humble smile.)

(The room quivers with soft mumbles. Listening carefully, Queen Brush thinks she hears "I'd rather sell wigs door-to-door," "I've always wanted to move to Lapland," and "I dunno.' I don't like those smart little creeps either!")

In 1895, Cesare Lombroso published a book entitled *The Man of Genius*. His main argument was that the "average man" is nature's ideal, and deviations toward better or worse—physically or mentally—are nature's mistakes. Citing specific famous persons as evidence, Lombroso wrote that "signs of degeneration in men of genius" included general emaciation, sickly color, rickets (which leads to club-footedness, lameness, or a hunched back), short stature, baldness, stuttering, forgetfulness, sterility, and that definite sign of brain degeneration—left-handedness!

His message was widely accepted, probably because Lombroso helped ordinary people feel much better about being ordinary.

Intellectually Gifted Students

Lombroso's seemingly authoritative book is the backdrop for the landmark 1925 Terman research mentioned briefly in Chapter 1. Before Terman, few questioned Lombroso's description of "men of genius" as physically and mentally inferior. Even today, some folks prefer to believe that intellectual superiority is accompanied by physical weakness and frequent illness.

But Terman found that, on average, children above Stanford-Binet IQ 135 (most above 140) were more psychologically stable, more socially adept, more physically fit, and even more attractive. In the words of Terman and Oden:

The average member of our group is a slightly better physical specimen than the average child....

...The superiority of gifted over unselected children was greater in reading, language usage, arithmetical reasoning, science, literature and the arts.

The interests of gifted children are many-sided and spontaneous, they learn to read easily and read more and better books than the average child. At the same time, they make numerous collections, cultivate many kinds of hobbies, and acquire far more knowledge of plays and games than the average child....

As compared with unselected children, they are less inclined to boast... they are more trustworthy when under temptation to cheat; their character preferences and social attitudes are more wholesome, and they score higher in a test of emotional stability....

> *The deviation of the gifted subjects from the generality is in the upward direction for nearly all traits. There is no law of compensation whereby the intellectual superiority of the gifted tends to be offset by inferiorities along nonintellectual lines.*[1]

Note that Terman and Oden's last sentence aimed directly at Lombroso's then-popular claims. Since Terman's early conclusions, countless others have studied characteristics of intellectually gifted children and adults at several (high) intelligence levels and with a variety of gifts and talents.

Some recurrent traits assembled from many sources appear in Table 2.1.[2] Of course, not all traits apply to all gifted children[3]—the reclusive young poet will hardly resemble the energetic and excitable math whiz. The poet-versus-math whiz example reflects Linda Silverman's distinction between visual-spatial versus auditory-sequential learners and thinkers, described later.[4]

Table 2.1. Common Characteristics of Gifted Students

Unusual alertness in infancy and later	Early and rapid learning
Rapid language development as a child	Superior language ability—verbally fluent, large vocabulary, complex grammar
Enjoys learning	Efficient, high-capacity memory
Academic superiority	Keen observation
Superior reasoning, problem solving	Imaginative, creative
High energy and enthusiasm	Good with numbers, puzzles
Preference for novelty	High curiosity, explores how and why
Insightful, sees "big picture," recognizes patterns, connects topics	Thinking that is abstract, complex, logical, insightful, flexible
Manipulates verbal, mathematical, artistic, or other symbol systems	Uses high-level thinking skills, efficient strategies
Wide interests, well-informed	Excellent sense of humor
Inquisitive, asks probing questions	Reflective
Extrapolates knowledge to new situations, goes beyond what is taught	Expanded awareness, greater self-awareness
Advanced interests	Multiple capabilities (multipotentiality)
High career ambitions	Overexcitability
Emotional intensity and sensitivity	High alertness and attention
High intellectual and physical activity level	High motivation, energetic, concentrates, perseveres, persists, task-oriented

High concentration, long attention span	Active—shares information, directs, leads, offers help, eager to be involved
Independent, self-directed, works alone	Aware of social issues, justice
Good self-concept, usually	Shows compassion for others
Prefers company of older students, adults	Strong empathy, moral thinking, sense of justice, honesty
Early and enthusiastic reader	

Further, subgroups of gifted students will show some characteristics and problems unique to their subgroup. As easy examples:

- Visual-spatial learners differ in their behaviors in many ways from auditory-sequential learners.

- Many, if not most, gifted African-American students experience peer pressure *not* to achieve ("Don't act White!").

- If the students live in poor homes, their high educational and career dreams can create uncomfortable conflicts with parents and siblings.

- In high school, female students' standardized math achievement scores run just slightly lower than males', and their English scores run slightly higher.

- Females' professional aspirations tend to decrease over the college years.

- Bright students with handicaps are regularly overlooked for gifted programs. One symptom of giftedness among handicapped gifted is *disruptiveness*—no doubt due to frustration at being treated like a dummy.[5]

- Gifted students in rural areas have decreased access to libraries, universities, and professional career models—as well as gifted programs—which lowers educational and career aspirations and opportunities.

Table 2.2 itemizes some characteristics of intellectual giftedness in preschool children. Most skills surpass those of typical kindergarten children; some surpass abilities of first-grade children.

Table 2.2. Characteristics Common to Gifted Preschool Children[6]

Speaks correctly in complex sentences
Uses comparatives ("This is like," "different from," "better than," "prettier than," etc.)
Uses connectives ("and," "but")
Sight reads familiar words and signs
Understands complex instructions
Has excellent memory for past events, spatial directions, etc.
Knows numbers
Counts well
Knows alphabet letters (in or out of order)
Sorts shapes
Solves jigsaw puzzles of 25 pieces or larger
Names many colors and shades

Returning to Table 2.1, the recurrent traits of gifted students look pretty good. In fact, many gifted children are studious, cooperative, and motivated in school. But other gifted children can show characteristics that are: (1) not helpful, (2) self-injurious, (3) puzzling and frustrating, and (4) irritating to teachers and parents. A short list of negative traits appears in Table 2.3.

Table 2.3. Problems and Negative Characteristics of Some Gifted Children

Uneven mental development in different cognitive areas
Underachievement, especially in uninteresting areas
Nonconformity, sometimes in disturbing directions
Interpersonal difficulties with less-able students
Self-doubt, poor self-image
Excessive self-criticism
Excessive sensitivity to feelings and expectations of others
Perfectionism, which can be extreme
Frustration and anger (e.g., from underdeveloped fine motor skills)
Depression
Rebelliousness, defiance, resistance to authority (e.g., verbally abusing a teacher)

Let's look more closely at some important categories of characteristics of gifted children and teenagers.

Precocious Language and Logical Thought

The most-often cited characteristic of gifted children is that, compared with average children of the same chronological age, they are ahead in language and thinking. They are precocious. Alfred Binet, who with Th. Simon developed the first successful intelligence test, coined the term *mental age*.[7] Mental age refers to the related ideas that: (1) children grow in intelligence, and (2) any given child may be mentally behind, equal to, or ahead of other children of the same age. A spin-off assumption is that at any given-age children who learn the fastest, learn the most, and grasp complex concepts and relationships more easily do so partly because of their higher intelligence.

Today, Binet's *mental age* concept has been refined by recognition of gifted children's *asynchronous development*.[8] That is, a gifted child's mental development simply is not "synchronized" in years (and months) with his or her (chronologically-controlled) physical development, and various mental abilities within a child may be quite uneven. A gifted child's thinking and analytic reasoning may be two, three, four, even six to 10 years ahead of other children of the same age, yet the child may be just keeping pace with age-mates in some of his or her other abilities.[9]

Of course, children differ, including gifted children. Some gifted children begin to talk at seven months. Others begin talking later but then may (or may not) progress rapidly. Gross described one extremely intelligent boy who did not begin talking unusually early, but according to his mother, once he did start talking, he jumped quickly from single words to complete sentences, with few pronunciation errors.[10]

The thinking of bright children tends to be quick and logical. Because of their curiosity, urge to learn, understanding of cause-effect relationships, insight, problem-solving ability, and persistence, such children may pester parents with "Why?" and "Why not?" questions. The bright and enthusiastic child may not accept such incomplete or illogical replies as "Just because!"

Early Art, Music, and Math Abilities

Children who are highly gifted in art possess remarkable and instinctive art skill.[11] They learn to draw at an early age, improve rapidly, have excellent visual memories, are obsessed with developing their art ability, and learn to solve problems dealing with perspective and necessary distortion (e.g., with distance or when viewed from different angles). Further, they learn virtually on their own. They even perceive their world in terms of shapes and visual surfaces, rather than more usual concepts.

Musical giftedness usually appears earlier than other varieties of gifts, perhaps at age one or two. A full 70% of great violinists were child prodigies—for example, Wolfgang Mozart and Yehudi Menuhin. An early clue is that very young musical prodigies tend to be fascinated by music. A musically gifted child may intuitively understand music structure, such as harmony and rhythm. The child may discriminate such expressive properties as timbre, phrasing, and loudness. A good "musical memory" allows the child to sing or play back a melody with an instrument, or perhaps transpose or improvise with a musical theme. One potential difficulty is that immature motor coordination can interfere with a musically gifted child's attempts to play an instrument like a guitar or clarinet.

A child gifted in mathematics might be adding and subtracting two-digit numbers and counting by fives and tens before kindergarten. Mathematical reasoning and insight also will be advanced. One second-grade child deduced the existence of negative numbers "because temperatures can go below zero."

Motivation and Persistence

While the logic is partly circular, a common characteristic of productive gifted students and distinguished adults is high motivation and persistence. In Terman's early research, high motivation—usually rooted in family values—was a key determiner of which of his bright children became successful and which did not.

Students at all ages must learn that "It's okay to fail. It's not okay to not try!"[12]

A common characteristic among gifted students is *perfectionism*.[13] Many feel that all projects and activities must be absolutely perfect. Despite the superior quality of their activities and output, perfectionistic students are predictably dissatisfied and frustrated to the point that it can impair their motivation and productivity.

Self-Confidence, Independence, Internal Control

After years of marvelous comments from parents, teachers, and peers—along with consistent success in school—it's hardly surprising that most gifted students become confident in themselves and willing to think and work independently.

The concept of *internal control,* which varies from low to high, refers to one's feelings of responsibility for successes, failures, and one's destiny. Gifted children tend to be high in internal control. They work hard, which they realize leads to success. Importantly, they use mistakes and failures constructively—they attribute their failures to inadequate effort, not low ability, which motivates them to do better next time.

External control is the reverse of internal control. Students high in *external control* are less likely to take credit (or blame) for successes (or failures). They might attribute school success to an easy task, a generous teacher, or good luck. And they might attribute failures to an unfair task, an unfair teacher, or just not feeling well. Note that neither successes nor failures motivate externally-controlled student to work harder.

Note also this seemingly curious problem. Internally-controlled gifted students may set high goals for themselves. If they happen to fail at these extra-high goals, their strong feelings of personal responsibility may cause them to believe that they are incompetent and stupid. Parents and teachers usually are baffled by the frustration and self-condemnation of such obviously capable students. The explanation is that such students are not comparing themselves with other students, but with their own high self-expectations.

Overexcitability, Emotional Giftedness, and Emotional Intelligence

The fascinating *overexcitability* syndrome is virtually unique to highly gifted students—and only to some of these. To understand over-excitability, the first step is to appreciate the unusual intensity of gifted children, as explained by psychologist Kazimierz Dabrowski. These overexcitabilities can explain what would otherwise be viewed as bizarre habits.

Dabrowski's Categories

Dabrowski originally identified five interrelated characteristics of overexcitability—namely, in the *psychomotor, intellectual, imaginational, sensual,* and *emotional* areas.[14] Such persons seem driven to raise their activity in *all five* areas to extraordinary levels.

And most of the time.

(1) *Psychomotor.* Behavior patterns in the psychomotor area are typically the first clue that a child, teenager, or adult may have the

overexcitability syndrome. The person shows an excess of energy, enthusiasm, drive, and restlessness; talks rapidly and compulsively; feels that he or she must take action, often impulsively; may bite fingernails or have other nervous habits; may be a workaholic; may enjoy fast games and sports; and may engage in delinquent activities.

A serious yet common problem in gifted education is differentiating between gifted students who are highly active—and many are—and gifted students who truly suffer from Attention Deficit Hyperactivity Disorder (ADHD), vaguely attributed to a still-unconfirmed brain disorder.[15] ADHD is characterized by poor attention, impulsiveness, and hyperactivity.

Far too often, gifted students are incorrectly diagnosed as having ADHD. For example, your author learned of one gifted class in which *half*(!) of the students were diagnosed as having ADHD. Many were taking Ritalin, a drug used to calm hyperactive children, prescribed by their pediatrician or a psychiatrist.

A built-in complication is that some gifted students *do* actually suffer from ADHD. For example, of 106 six- to nine-year-old gifted children in China, 10 truly did have ADHD.[16]

(2) *Intellectual.* Common student behavior in the intellectual overexcitability area includes high levels of curiosity, questioning, analysis, and discovery. Such students enjoy ideas and a search for truth. Their learning habits include extensive reading, high concentration, asking probing questions, solving problems, integrating concepts, thinking about thinking (metacognition), and a preoccupation with problems in specific areas.

The intellectual area includes high levels of moral thinking—for example, pondering the morality of war—which includes acquiring *universal values*, moral guides that are good for everyone independent of authority (e.g., kindness, patience, fairness, honesty, truthfulness, and concern for others).[17]

(3) *Imaginational.* The imaginational component of overexcitability means high creativity. Excitable and sensitive gifted students let their imaginations run. They engage in fantasy, strong visual imagery, magical thinking (e.g., paranormal, psychical), dreams,

metaphorical thinking, and often poetry. Truth may mix with fiction. Due to their lively imaginations, they may experience a greater fear of the (imagined) unknown.

(4) *Sensual.* The sensual area includes pleasure in seeing, tasting, smelling, touching, and hearing. The sensual category may include buying sprees, overeating, frequent masturbation, and other sexual experiences.

(5) *Emotional.* The emotional category of overexcitability includes intense positive and negative feelings—soaring highs and dismal lows. "Highs" include feeling fantastically alive and incredibly energetic, both wrapped in waves of joy. The "lows" in the emotional area can include such physical and psychological symptoms as a tense stomach, flushing, a "sinking heart," high anxiety, shyness, feelings of guilt, depression, self-criticism, feelings of inadequacy and inferiority, concern with death, and even suicidal moods.

The first three of Dabrowski's characteristics of overexcitability—high energy (*psychomotor*), thirst for knowledge (*intellectual*), and high creativity (*imaginational*)—especially contribute to the high achievement and accomplishments of gifted students.

Emotional Giftedness

The topic of *overexcitability*—especially the subtopics of *intellectual* and *emotional excitability*—overlap with the separate but closely related broad topic labeled *emotional giftedness.* A prime characteristic of emotional giftedness is extraordinary levels of empathy, moral thinking, awareness, and sensitivity. Emotionally gifted students tend to hold universal values—values that apply to all people. They show deep concern for others' rights and feelings, as well as high sensitivity to social issues, especially if the issues involve unfairness and injustice.

In Annemarie Roeper's opinion, gifted children differ more from each other emotionally than they do cognitively.[18]

Linda Silverman described emotionally gifted—intense and sensitive—children as those who were doing things like:

Fighting injustice, befriending and protecting handicapped children, conserving resources, becoming terribly upset if a classmate is humiliated, becoming vegetarian in meat-eating families, crying at the violence in cartoons, being perplexed at why classmates push in line…writing letters to the president to try to end the war, and writing poems of anguish at the cruelty in the world.[19]

Emotional Intelligence

In Joyce VanTassel-Baska's vocabulary, *emotional intelligence* is gifted students' keen ability to perceive and express emotions, understand and use emotions, and manage emotions to foster their personality growth.[20] As components of emotional intelligence, *emotional understanding* is gifted students' better comprehension of such topics as terrorism and homelessness, and their ability to apply their understanding of emotions to, for example, creative writing and bibliotherapy.[21] *Managing emotion* refers to regulating and controlling one's own emotions, plus helping others deal with their emotions.

Emotional giftedness? Emotional intelligence? Overexcitability? ADHD? Dabrowski, VanTassel-Baska, Silverman, and Roeper? The reader may easily confuse these similar labels, overlapping definitions and concepts, and their authors.

One more.

Emotional Intelligence is the title of a best-selling 1995 book by Daniel Goleman. Drawing from other authors' ethical considerations, Goleman's title refers to good character, good "moral instincts," and ethical and sensible interpersonal behavior. Goleman argues that emotional intelligence is mostly independent of IQ—which measures verbal and math skills—and much more important. As a bonus, while IQ is mostly fixed, emotional intelligence can be taught and learned.

High emotional intelligence includes self-awareness, self-control, persistence, high self-motivation, altruism, and lots of empathy. All are skills that should be taught to children. Persons high in emotional intelligence are able to read others' feelings and emotions. They handle relationships well. They likely are successful at work.

Low emotional intelligence seems to be a world-wide trend. Self-control is absent. Moral deficiency replaces rationality. Further, low emotional intelligence includes loneliness, depression, anger, unruliness, nervousness, worrying, impulsiveness, aggression, selfishness, violence, mean-spiritedness, rage, despair, desperation, recklessness, drug use, and even eating disorders. Low emotional intelligence is visible in child abuse and abandonment, school and freeway shootings, and domestic violence.

Bright people can do dumb things. After quoting Clint Eastwood's threatening "Make my day!," Goleman quotes Aristotle, who neatly summarized the matter in about 310 BC:

Anyone can become angry—that is easy. But to be angry with the right person, to the right degree, at the right time, for the right purpose, and in the right way—this is not easy.[22]

Overall, the topics of emotional giftedness and emotional intelligence suggest marvelous potential for moral leadership and inspiration. One good recommendation is that teachers infuse affective/emotional components into the curriculum for gifted students.[23]

A problem might be finding teachers—or parents—who understand the dynamics of overexcitability and emotional giftedness. Intimately related difficulties, noted Roeper, are parents who emphasize sports and just want their children to be normal, and teachers who just want to get students ready for the next grade.[24]

Visual-Spatial Learners

Psychologists have long been aware of the distinction between *visual-spatial learning and thinking* (non–logical, non-sequential, nonverbal, non-analytic) versus *auditory-sequential learning and thinking* (the reverse).[25] Visual-spatial thinking traditionally is associated with the right brain hemisphere, auditory-sequential thinking with the left hemisphere. The two tendencies lie at opposite ends of a continuum, with most of us somewhere in between. According to Silverman, about one-third of all persons may be visual-spatial learners and thinkers.

Silverman's 2002 book *Upside-Down Brilliance: The Visual-Spatial Learner* described many, many important differences between visual-spatial learners versus auditory-sequential learners. Her conclusions stemmed from studies of gifted children, children with learning disabilities (e.g., dyslexia), brain research, and other sources. As two examples, visual-spatial children can get into trouble for producing a math answer without knowing how they did it, or for not following a teacher's (sequential) instructions. Such children do poorly on verbal portions of ability tests.

Some characteristics of visual-spatial learners and contrasting traits of auditory-sequential learners appear in Table 2.4.[26]

Table 2.4. Some Characteristics of Visual-Spatial Learners and Auditory-Sequential Learners[27]

Visual-Spatial Learners:
○ Think in images rather than words
○ May need time to verbally express ideas
○ Find patterns and perceive wholes quickly
○ Understand suddenly with "Aha!" experiences; are good synthesizers
○ See the "big picture" or patterns, but may miss details
○ Are good observers
○ Learn from direct experience, seeing, intuition, and imagery
○ Prefer to read maps rather than get verbal directions
○ Remember what they see, forget what they hear
○ Can visualize objects from different perspectives
○ Must visualize words in order to spell them
○ Have poor handwriting
○ Are poor at spelling
○ May have uneven grades
○ Read maps well
○ Solve problems in unusual ways
○ Have poor time sense—schedules and deadlines are difficult
○ Cannot explain how they know things
○ Do not separate thinking and emotion
○ Are more emotionally sensitive
○ Empathize with others' feelings
○ Are more sensitive to teachers' attitudes
○ Are good at artistic, musical, and mechanical activities
○ Have vivid imaginations
○ Are creative thinkers
○ May experience the "imposter syndrome"—they believe that they are not as smart as others think because they do not dominate discussions, are not quick thinkers, do not know where their ideas come from, and in school could not show their work
○ Feel smarter as they get older
○ Strongly dislike speaking to groups

Visual-Spatial Learners (continued):
○ Strongly like their computer (which has a spell checker and compensates for poor handwriting!)
○ Are late bloomers

Auditory-Sequential Learners:
○ Think in words more than images
○ Are step-by-step learners
○ Attend to details
○ Are good listeners
○ Follow instructions well
○ Learn well in sequential, step-by-step fashion
○ Sound out spelling words
○ Have good handwriting
○ Can show steps of work
○ Are good at verbal expression
○ Process information rapidly
○ Can separate thinking and reasoning from emotion
○ Are early bloomers

Humor

Most gifted children have a strong sense of humor, which follows from their general self-confidence and abilities to think quickly and see relationships. In school, the humor may appear in creative writing or art projects. One bright child locked his mother out of the house. She yelled for him to "Open the door!" So he walked with a grin into the kitchen and opened the refrigerator. A teacher asked an IQ 158 boy, who enjoyed puns and wordplay, "Can you pass that cup, please?" He placed the cup on the floor and soberly walked back and forth "past" the cup.

Raisin' Brains: Surviving My Smart Family is a hysterically funny—and at 183 pages, readably short—book by Karen Isaacson that presents lots of first-hand insights into the nature of giftedness and creativity. The book colorfully describes episodes with the author's five gifted children, plus her own gifted mom who "let my sisters push her around in a grocery cart at the supermarket...[and] while everybody else's mother was singing them to sleep with lullabies, my mother was singing us to sleep with 'Why'd I Eat Those Worms?'"—a tune that includes "sucking the guts out."[28] Said Isaacson, "Creativity is a kid's best friend. It's what got Myron and Gertrude and me through summers of bitter dandelion leaf salad when we were playing pioneers and decided to live off the land."[29]

At nine months, before he could walk, Isaacson's son Stanley—described as "hungry for information"—learned some alphabet letters by watching *Sesame Street*©. (Isaacson claimed not to know that there *was* an alphabet until she was six.) By 18 months, Stanley had learned all of the basic shapes and numbers and the entire alphabet. Before age three, he could read the newspaper. He particularly liked the movie section and soon became "a walking movie encyclopedia."[30]

Regarding testing for giftedness: "Meanwhile, back at the Stone Age, there they are, gathered around this lovely, warm, new light and heat source, and one of them is sitting on a rock, sucking on a burnt finger. He's what we call the 'test administrator.' He now knows that the fire is hot.... Does he know exactly how hot it is?... Nope, but he knows it's hot. IQ and ability tests operate on the same principle. You won't get an absolutely accurate reading, but you'll be able to recognize definite areas of strength and weakness, and you'll know there are some things happening in that child's brain that are well above average thinking temperature."[31]

Informal Evaluation: Annemarie Roeper

Before retiring to El Cerrito, California, to create Roeper Consultation Services, Annemarie Roeper was the founder and leader of her (continuing) Roeper School for gifted children in Bloomfield Hills, Michigan. She also created the *Roeper Review*, a leading journal in gifted education.

Roeper's informal evaluation of gifted students' characteristics began with parent interviews. She listened to the parents' description of their child and learned the parents' views and "emotional feelings" about giftedness.

Her unique method of evaluating and getting to know the students—acquiring "pure" information—reached beyond ability tests. After the parent interview, Roeper went for a walk with each child. She would learn who was great at math, who had a great imagination, how well they spoke, how sensitive they were, how gifted they were, how much freedom they had been given, what kinds of friends they had, and what the child's interests were.

Roeper presented many personality-related gems at the 2004 National Association for Gifted Children (NAGC) meeting in Salt Lake

City. For example, early in her career a logical question was: "How can I make children adjust to school?" Over the years, the question became: "How can I make the school adjust to each gifted child?" Roeper felt that she must match the learning environment to the child.

Initially, Roeper considered herself a realist: laws of physics govern our world, and what you see is what exists. Her work with gifted children changed her beliefs. Truth and reality, she now believes, are relative—relative to children's thinking, sensitivity, and perceptions. For example, the expanded senses of some gifted children permit them to hear, see, and feel things that the rest of us cannot experience. Many— not just one or two—believe that rocks, trees, flowers, and the earth are alive: "There are children who hug trees and are inconsolable if we cut them down."[32] Roeper—but I confess not your author—claims that their expanded reality, which she sometimes calls *spiritual reality*, includes ESP, memories of past lives, déjà vu experiences, and prenatal memories, along with their enhanced senses. A child who "constantly wears his jacket and keeps his hood over his head may be trying to keep out the bombardment of other people's feelings and expectations."[33] A child who hums constantly may be expressing inner tension. One child's sense of touch was so keen that he preferred not to wear clothes because of the discomfort.

"The more highly gifted they are, the more they live in a different world than we do," said Roeper.[34] They often do not fit well with class- mates. Many think something is wrong with them, a fairly common problem among the highly gifted. They need to feel that the teacher is on their side.

In agreement, other gifted experts have noted that we must be open to the worlds of gifted children.[35] We must give them time to talk about what it's like being gifted.

Gifted Underachievement

As a group, bright children normally do not underachieve in school. But some do. This self-contradictory puzzle frustrates parents, teachers, and school counselors. Sometimes the underachievement is due to phys- ical, mental, or emotional problems.[36] For example, the underachieving gifted student may have a hearing problem, ADHD, or upsetting home difficulties.

When these problems are eliminated, McCoach and Siegle noted that gifted underachievement has been attributed to one or more of the following four factors.

(1) *Low self-perceived academic ability.* Students' academic self-concepts might influence their selection of learning activities, how much they challenge themselves, and their academic persistence.

(2) *Negative attitudes toward school, teachers, and/or classes.* Students who succeed in school presumably are interested in and positive about school and schoolwork. Underachieving students might have problems with authority, including teachers, other school personnel, and classes themselves.

(3) *Poor self-management and low motivation.* Self-management, which is intertwined with motivation, refers to a student's control of effort and learning strategies. Academic problems can be due to poor self-management skills.

(4) *Low perceived value and importance of school learning.* Students who fail to see the long-term value and usefulness of school learning are more likely to underachieve.

McCoach and Siegle tried to untangle the gifted/underachievement puzzle by comparing 122 gifted achievers with 56 gifted underachievers from high schools around the U.S. *Gifted* meant IQ or achievement scores above the 92nd percentile. Using McCoach's *School Attitude Assessment Survey-Revised*, they first confirmed a common trend in gender differences—they found three times as many male high school underachievers as female underachievers.

Regarding factor 1 above—self-perceptions of academic ability—McCoach and Siegle discovered that both gifted achievers *and* gifted underachievers in high school perceived themselves as having high academic ability. Both groups of students knew they were smart, and both groups knew they possessed the skills and abilities to succeed.

So much for factor 1, low self-perceived academic ability.

Regarding the other three factors, differences between achievers and underachievers were whopping—all favoring achievers. The achievers held better attitudes toward school, teachers, and classes. Their motivation and self-management skills were stronger. And achievers valued school learning more highly.

Explanation of "whopping": Remember standard deviations from Chapter 1? The differences between achievers and underachievers averaged about *one standard deviation*. The two largest differences between achievers and underachievers were on the *poor self-management and low motivation* scales and the *value and importance of school learning* scales. For example, the average rating on 7-point scales evaluating motivation and self-management was 5.48 for achievers, but just 3.90 for underachievers.

Desirable Characteristics of Teachers of the Gifted

We should not only understand common, recurrent characteristics of gifted children, we also should be aware of desirable characteristics of effective teachers of the gifted. The two topics mesh in at least one obvious way: *good teachers of gifted students should be gifted themselves.* Such kinship helps empathy, understanding, and communication. Also, *whatever* the program arrangement—acceleration, enrichment, grouping, or a combination of these—enthusiastic and well-qualified teachers will make or break a gifted program.

Desirable characteristics of teachers of the gifted appear in Table 2.5. Of course, knowledge and competencies needed to teach students gifted in specific areas—science, math, physics, art, music, literature—will differ between teachers.

Table 2.5. Desirable Characteristics of Teachers of the Gifted[37]

Exemplary Teachers of the Gifted:
○ Understand and empathize with gifted students.
○ Are highly intelligent.
○ Are competent in the content area.
○ Are enthusiastic about giftedness, talent, and learning.
○ Align more closely with gifted students than do more formal teachers.
○ Are aware of gifted students' needs.
○ Have confidence in gifted students.
○ Eagerly back acceleration options.
○ Are energetic, ready to do extra work, and ready to experiment.
○ Are imaginative, innovative, flexible, and open to change.
○ Are capable of modifying a curriculum.

Exemplary Teachers of the Gifted (continued):
○ Are capable of organizing and managing classroom activities.
○ Are honest, fair, and objective.
○ Are patient, sensitive, and respectful.
○ Recognize individual differences, including personal self-images.
○ Accept responsibility for each single student.
○ Are less judgmental and critical than most teachers.
○ Create a vibrant, warm, safe, and democratic learning environment.
○ Are willing to learn with and from students.
○ Are lifelong learners—"perennial students"—themselves.
○ Have broad general knowledge.
○ Have cultural and intellectual interests.
○ Are mature, experienced, and self-confident.
○ Have control over their personal lives.
○ Can work closely with other members of the gifted staff, students, parents, and other professionals.
○ Can communicate the needs of gifted children and muster support for the gifted program.

A study by Mills examined characteristics of 63 unusually effective teachers of the gifted in Julian Stanley's Center for Talented Youth (CTY) summer programs.[38] These expert teachers had taught at CTY for at least two summers and were nominated as "exemplary" by CTY administrators. Students also had a vote. The talented CTY seventh graders gave these teachers high ratings in "knowledge of content, preparedness, concern for individual learning, and openness to differing opinions."[39]

As for biographical characteristics, most exemplary teachers had taught at CTY for over four years and had about eight years' experience teaching gifted students. No surprises so far, but keep reading. Nearly 80% had never taken a course in gifted education. Only 32% were certified to teach. The latter surprise actually makes sense, since 85% had master's or doctorate degrees and two-thirds were college instructors.

The exemplary teachers also took the *Myers-Briggs Personality Inventory*. Compared with average middle-school teachers, the outstanding CTY teachers of the gifted scored about the same on both the *Extroversion-Introversion* scale and the *Judging* (orderly)–*Perceiving* (flexibility) scale. However, on the *Sensing* (factual, practical)-*Intuition* scale, the CTY teachers scored much higher on *intuition* than did middle school teachers. Also, on the *Thinking-Feeling* scale, the CTY teachers scored much higher on *thinking*.

In sum—and despite their usual lack of education courses or teacher certification—these highly effective teachers of the gifted were well educated, knowledgeable in their subject area, highly interested in student learning and student opinions, strong in intuition and thinking, and had many years' experience teaching gifted students.

Summary

- Lombroso's 1895 book proposed that "men of genius" are nature's mistakes and show degeneration of various types.

- However, Terman found that highly intelligent children and adolescents, on average, were superior physically, were better in school subjects, read more, had more interests and hobbies, and were more trustworthy and emotionally stable.

- Further, Table 2.1 lists more than 40 common (and usually superior) characteristics of gifted students—for example, early and rapid learning, superior reasoning, high curiosity, wide and advanced interests, greater self-awareness, independence, creativity, and a good sense of humor.

- Subgroups of gifted also show traits and problems peculiar to their group—for example, studious African-American students are accused of "acting White," young women's aspirations decrease over the college years, gifted handicapped students are overlooked for gifted programs, and rural gifted students have less access to libraries, gifted programs, universities, and more.

- Abilities of gifted preschoolers may surpass those of average kindergartners and even first graders.

- Negative traits include, for example, underachievement in uninteresting areas, self-criticism, excessive sensitivity to others' feelings and expectations, perfectionism, frustration, depression, and rebelliousness.

- Characteristics of the gifted include precocious language and logic; their mental development is typically not synchronized with their physical development.

- The artistically gifted may learn to draw early, improve rapidly, have superior visual memory, and solve artistic problems (e.g., perspective). Musical giftedness may appear at age one or two. A mathematically gifted child might add, subtract, and count by fives or tens before kindergarten.

- Not surprisingly, a common trait of productive students and successful adults is strong motivation and persistence.

- Years of success lead to self-confidence and a willingness to work independently.

- Gifted children tend to be high in internal control. They use mistakes and failures constructively. With failure, strong feelings of personal responsibility may lead to feelings of incompetence and stupidity.

- Overexcitability is unique to some highly gifted students. It includes the five sub-areas of: (1) psychomotor, characterized by, for example, high activity and energy, sometimes mistaken for ADHD; (2) intellectual, including, for example, curiosity, extensive reading, metathinking, and high moral thinking; (3) imaginational, referring to high creativity and sometimes including fear of the unknown; (4) sensual, referring to pleasure in seeing, tasting, smelling, touching, and hearing; and (5) emotional, including intense highs and lows.

- *Emotional giftedness* includes high levels of empathy, moral thinking, and awareness. It also includes sensitivity to social issues and high concern for others.

- Silverman said that emotionally gifted children are intense and sensitive—they befriend handicapped children, conserve resources, and may ask the U.S. President to end poverty.

- According to VanTassel-Baska, *emotional intelligence* is the ability to perceive, express, understand, and use emotions. *Emotional understanding* refers to comprehending, for example, terrorism and homelessness, and applying knowledge of emotions in creative writing.

- Daniel Goleman explained that emotional intelligence—which is independent of IQ—includes good character, self-awareness, good moral instincts, and ethical behavior.

- Teachers should infuse affective and emotional components into the gifted curriculum to promote moral leadership.

- In contrast with auditory-sequential learners, visual-spatial learners think in images instead of words, perceive patterns and wholes quickly, see the "big picture" but miss details, prefer maps to verbal directions, have poor handwriting and spelling, are more emotionally sensitive, and are more creative.

- Most gifted children have a strong sense of humor.

- *Raisin' Brains* by Karen Isaacson humorously describes life with gifted children, plus a gifted mom, that illustrates many insights into giftedness and creativity.

- Annemarie Roeper, creator of the Roeper School for gifted children and the *Roeper Review,* evaluated school candidates using informal walks and chats. She came to accept the expanded senses and sensitivity of gifted children, including their reports of ESP, prenatal memories, and more.

- Underachievement in gifted students may be due to physical (e.g., hearing), mental (e.g., ADHD), or emotional (e.g., family) problems. Four other factors are low self-perceived academic ability, negative attitudes toward school and teachers, poor self-management or low motivation, and low perceived value and importance of school learning.

- McCoach and Siegle found that achievers and underachievers did not differ in self-perceived academic ability. But underachievers did hold negative attitudes toward teachers, classes, and school; had low motivation and poor self-management skills; and did not value school learning.

- Good teachers of the gifted, above all, should be gifted themselves. They also should be enthusiastic about giftedness, aware of gifted students' needs, imaginative, flexible, fair, sensitive, respectful, and have wide general knowledge and intellectual interests.

- A study of exemplary teachers at Julian Stanley's CTY summer program indicated that they had at least four years' experience at CTY—but 80% had never taken a gifted course, and just one-third were certified to teach. Most held master's or doctorate degrees. On the *Myers-Briggs Personality Inventory*, they scored high on intuition (rather than sensing) and thinking (rather than feeling).

3
Definitions, Theories, and Legal Questions

Nowadays, a look through the relevant literature pertaining
to giftedness can be quite confusing due to the amazing
variety of definitions for giftedness or gifted persons.
~ Albert Ziegler and Kurt A. Heller

[**Scene**: *Austrian courtroom in 1930. Judge Wilhelm Wilhangum is reading the* *charges against defendant Sigmund Freud.*]

Judge Wilhelm Wilhangum: Herr Doktor Freud, you bin charged mit using schmutty ideas in your theory about schtudents who are schmart und gifted. How do you plead, you guilty know-it-alles?

Sigmund Freud: I bin not guilty, Judge! I bin writin' und speakin' only die truth!

Judge: But die truth is, you bin sayin' dot boy schtudents are schmart und gifted und all dat because they vant to make hay mit der mamas! Und die same for girls und der papas! I tink das ist schmutty, Herr Freud!

Freud: But Judge, dot isn't schmutty! Dot ist die Oedipus complex! Ich invented it in 1910! Terman chust invented gifted kinder in 1925! Beside, don't you luff your mama? Don't you kiss your mama? Don't you vish daddy would trip on das coal bucket?

Judge: Of course I luff my mama. Everybody luffs der mama. But nobody vant's der daddy to trip on das coal bucket!

Freud: I tink you bin repressin' your fantasies about sluggin' your papa! Maybe you chust kick a doggie vunce in a vile!

Judge: Sounds fischy to me, Herr Freud. Are you sure?

Freud: Am I not die world's greatest psychoanalyst?

Judge: Maybe so. But I sink I give you six months in das slammer anyvay to clean up your theory!

Freud: I sink you love your mama, hate your papa, und you bin pickin' on defenseless psychoanalysts!

Judge: Make dot a year.

There are no universally-accepted definitions of *gifted*, *talented*, or *gifted and talented*.[1] It is common to use the terms *gifted* and *talented* interchangeably—we might refer to the same student as a gifted chess player (or artist, or math student) or a talented chess player (or artist, or math student). Also, the single word *gifted* can substitute for the slightly more cumbersome "gifted and talented," as when we refer in conversation to a school's "gifted program" or "gifted teacher."

Implications of Formal Definitions

The formal definition of *gifted and talented* endorsed by a state, school district, or individual school has important policy, procedural, and social implications. For example:

The definition will guide the identification procedure; it will decide who is or is not admitted to the program—that is, *who is or is not gifted*.

The definition will influence the content and procedures of the program itself—in other words, what and how the gifted students are taught. We will see that most definitions are reasonably broad. A broad definition implicitly requires broad opportunities for self-selected independent research, art, or other projects, in addition to greater subject depth or subject acceleration—for example, in math, art, or social studies.

As a danger, the definition of *gifted and talented* (e.g., tested IQ above 130) and its consequent identification methods might discriminate against subgroups, such as poor, minority, underachieving, and even female students.

Accepting a student into a G/T program, according to the local definition, automatically labels that student as "gifted." Positive effects of such labeling include improvements in self-esteem, self-expectations, and academic motivation.

Defining, identifying, and labeling some students as "gifted" can alienate classmates, the classmates' parents, and (usually temporarily) the gifted students' own brothers and sisters.

Students not selected, of course, miss opportunities for academic and leadership development. Further, non-selection may lower their self-esteem, self-concepts, and self-expectations. After all, "I'm not gifted!"

As mentioned in Chapter 1, some students will barely reach the IQ, achievement, and/or teacher recommendation criteria, while others might be off the scale—for example, with tested IQ scores of 150 or higher, remarkable artistic or poetic ability, or extreme depth and capability in an academic area. There is no accepted term that distinguishes such stellar students from others in a G/T program, although we hear the label "extremely gifted" and tongue-in-cheek terms like "severely gifted," "profoundly gifted," and "terminally gifted."

As other thoughts on defining *gifted and talented*, gifted education leaders Cox, Daniel, and Boston prefer the less pompous-sounding term *able learners.*[2] Others object to bestowing the title "gifted and talented" solely as a result of the identification process. They might prefer the phrase "potentially gifted." G/T leader Joseph Renzulli recommends not referring to "gifted students," but to "students with gifted behaviors," which may be developed in special programs.[3]

The Federal Definition

Beginning in 1972, the U.S. Office of Education created a sensible definition of *gifted and talented*, which was revised slightly in 1978 and 1988.[4] The one-sentence 1988 version reads:

> *The term "gifted and talented students" means children and youth who give evidence of high performance capability in areas such as intellectual, creative, artistic [visual and performing], or leadership capacity, or in specific academic fields, and who require services or activities not ordinarily provided by the school in order to fully develop such capabilities.*

Note that the definition includes not only high general intelligence, but high ability in specific academic areas as well. Further, it recognizes giftedness in nonacademic areas, namely creativity, the arts, and leadership. The phrase "give evidence of high performance capability" suggests that underachieving gifted students should be identified—for example, underachieving minority gifted. (The original 1972 version used the phrase "demonstrated achievement and/or potential ability," which more clearly refers to underachieving gifted students.)

What is critical is that the U.S.O.E definition specifies that such gifted and talented students require special activities and services (i.e., programs, counseling) beyond normal school programs.

In view of its authoritativeness, most states—and school districts—include the gist of the U.S.O.E. definition in their own state and district definitions of *gifted and talented*. Regrettably, some programs that officially endorse the U.S.O.E. definition continue to give most weight to IQ scores and grades in their actual selection procedures—and ignore creativity, artistic abilities, and leadership capability.

Three-Ring Model of Giftedness: Joseph Renzulli

Joseph Renzulli currently is one of America's most influential and productive scholars in gifted education.[5] At his National Research Center on the Gifted and Talented (NRCG/T) at the University of Connecticut, Renzulli and Sally Reis have directed or overseen continuous school-based research on key problems in gifted education. For example, there are ongoing NRCG/T projects aimed at clarifying:

- Effective techniques for training G/T teachers and staff.

- Fair identification procedures.

- Effective program practices.

- Giftedness in special populations.

- Standards for G/T teacher certification.

- Methods and effects of curriculum compacting (eliminating already-mastered material).

- Financial and administrative policies and staff training activities for schools with various socio-economic, ethnic, handicapped, and geographic (e.g., isolated) G/T students.

For now, we are concerned with Renzulli's definition of giftedness, mentioned briefly in Chapter 1. His *three-ring model* is based on descriptions of eminent, creatively productive persons who have made notable contributions to society. The gifted behavior of such persons results from an interaction among three characteristics: *high creativity, high task commitment* (i.e., motivation), and at least *above average* (not necessarily outstanding) *intellectual ability.* Renzulli's popular model is summarized as three overlapping circles (Figure 3.1).

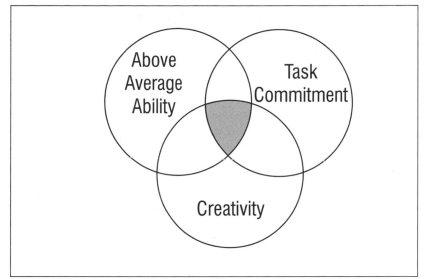

Figure 3.1. Renzulli's three-ring model. Reprinted by permission of the author.

Unfortunately, some G/T program directors or teachers have mistakenly used Renzulli's three-ring model as a guide for identifying students. After all, they reason, if these three traits define giftedness, that's what we oughta' look for. An honest mistake. We will see in Chapter 4 that Renzulli recommends an unusually sensible selection procedure that differs substantially from his three-ring definition of giftedness.

Multiple-Intelligence Theory: Howard Gardner

Harvard psychologist Howard Gardner probably did not intend to produce an influential definition/theory of giftedness. But he did. His base argument is simply that there is more to intelligence than a single IQ number, a proposition that is widely accepted by G/T scholars and teachers. His initial *multiple-intelligence theory* identified seven types of intelligence.[6] He added an eighth in 1999 (item 8, below).

Note that intelligence types 1 and 2—*linguistic* and *logical-mathematical*—are both highly valued by educators and measured by intelligence tests.

(1) *Linguistic intelligence* refers to, for example, verbal comprehension, semantics, and oral and written expression, as needed by lawyers and novelists.

(2) *Logical-mathematical intelligence* includes computing ability and inductive and deductive reasoning, as necessary for mathematicians and physicists.

(3) *Spatial intelligence,* most centrally, is the ability to mentally manipulate three-dimensional configurations, as by architects, sculptors, interior decorators, engineers, and chess players.

(4) *Musical intelligence* includes, for example, sensitivity to rhythm and timbre, pitch discrimination, and the abilities to perform and compose music.

(5) *Bodily-kinesthetic intelligence* refers to controlling all or part of one's body to execute movements, as needed by dancers and athletes.

(6) *Interpersonal intelligence*—social skills—includes the ability to understand others' motivations and actions and to respond logically to that information, as required by politicians, evangelists, counselors, and teachers.

(7) *Intrapersonal intelligence* refers to understanding one's own strengths, weaknesses, feelings, and emotions, as when a child admits, "I like to play soccer, but I'm not very good at it."

(8) *Naturalist intelligence,* at high levels, refers to a broad knowledge of taxonomies of living things—a capability to recognize and classify animals and plants.

Teachers acquainted with Gardner's explanation of intelligence should take a wider and more informed view of student intelligence. The one or two numbers from the Stanford-Binet and Wechsler tests do not explain the total picture.

Gardner is still considering adding more types of intelligence to his list.

Triarchic Theory: Robert Sternberg

Sometimes called his *theory of successful intelligence,* Robert Sternberg created a three-part theory that, like Gardner's, presents an alternative to describing intelligence with a single IQ number.[7]

In his triarchic theory, Sternberg's *analytic giftedness* is basic academic ability. It is measured by intelligence tests, especially tests of reading comprehension and analytical reasoning.

Synthetic giftedness refers to creativity. Sternberg includes the concepts of intuition, insightfulness, and coping well with novelty. Noted Sternberg, synthetic thinkers may not have the highest IQ scores, but they are likely to make unique and valuable contributions to society.

Practical giftedness is the ability to apply analytic and synthetic giftedness to everyday situations. In a new environment, practical giftedness helps one figure out what to do and how to do it.

In minimal words, a student may be smart, creative, or able (and motivated) to use his or her smarts and creativity to get things done.

Apparently as an insightful afterthought, Sternberg realized that evil leaders (e.g., Hitler, Osama bin Laden, Saddam Hussein) must be remarkably high in practical giftedness.[8] He added *wisdom* as a subtype of practical giftedness, naming Mother Theresa, Gandhi, and Martin Luther King, Jr. as positive examples.

Sternberg presented his three main types, or sets, of thinking skills just slightly differently in 2000.[9] *Analytic giftedness* became *critical thinking,* essentially a synonym, and it includes the specifics of analyzing, critiquing, judging, evaluating, comparing and contrasting, and assessing. *Synthetic giftedness* became *creative thinking,* again a synonym, and includes creating, discovering, inventing, imagining, supposing, and hypothesizing. *Practical giftedness* (using the same name as in 1997 and 2003) includes applying, utilizing, and practicing.

Compare Sternberg's triarchic theory of intelligence with Renzulli's three-ring model of giftedness. Similarities? Differences?

Multiple-Talent Totem Poles: Calvin Taylor

Calvin Taylor's *multiple-talent totem pole* concept raises our awareness that almost all students will have above-average skills or talents of some type.[10] His 1984 model appears in Figure 3.2. Note that if we look at traditional *academic* ability, Ann—who also tops the *productive thinking* totem pole—is the natural choice for the gifted program. But if we look at *planning* (organizing, designing) talent, Randy would be top choice. Kathy tops the totem pole in both *communicating* (speaking, writing) and *decision-making* (weighing information, making good choices).

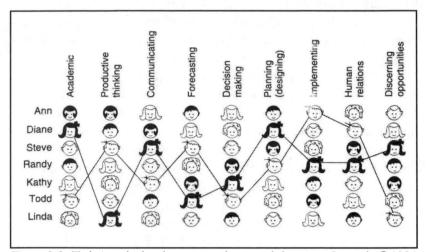

Figure 3.2. Taylor's multiple-talent totem poles, extended version. Copyright ©1984, Calvin W. Taylor. Reprinted by permission.

How do we define *gifted and talented*? Who do we select for the school gifted program? Taylor's model of giftedness may be viewed as an eye-opening guide to perceiving, guiding, and teaching all children.

Who, What, and How of Giftedness: Abraham Tannenbaum

Abraham Tannenbaum defined giftedness with an eight-category model that looks at *who, what,* and *how* questions.[11] His model is summarized in Figure 3.1. Note, first, that the model implicitly stresses both high intelligence (persons who are "proficient") and high creativity. Second, as illustrated in his own examples, the model focuses on *adults* who are highly creative or proficient. Tannenbaum argues that the model helps understand childhood potential for becoming a gifted adult based on answers to the *who, what,* and *how* questions.